Nail
Art &
Design

Nail
Art &
Design

Tammy Bigan

Milady Publishing Company
(A Division of Delmar Publishers Inc.)

Notice to the Reader

Publisher does not warrant or guarantee any of the products described herein or perform any independent analysis in connection with any of the product information contained herein. Publisher does not assume, and expressly disclaims, any obligation to obtain and include information other than that provided to it by the manufacturer. The reader is expressly warned to consider and adopt all safety precautions that might be indicated by the activities described herein and to avoid all potential hazards. By following the instructions contained herein, the reader willingly assumes all risks in connection with such instructions.

The publisher makes no representations or warranties of any kind, including but not limited to, the warranties of fitness for particular purpose or merchantability, nor are any such representations implied with respect to the material set forth herein, and the publisher takes no responsibility with respect to such material. The publisher shall not be liable for any special, consequential or exemplary damages resulting, in whole or in part, from the readers' use of, or reliance upon, this material.

Credits:

Publisher: Catherine Frangie
Developmental Editor: Laura V. Miller
Production Manager: John Mickelbank

Freelance Project Editor: Gail Hamrick
Photography by: Steven Paul Knox

Cover Design by: design M design W
Cover Photos by: Steven Paul Knox
Text Design by: design M design W

For information address:
Milady Publishing Company
(A Division of Delmar Publishers Inc.)
3 Columbia Circle, Box 12519
Albany, NY 12212-2519

Printed in the United States of America
Published simultaneously in Canada
by Nelson Canada
a Division of The Thomson Corporation

3   4   5   6   7   8   9   10   XXX   00   99   98

Library of Congress Cataloging-in-Publication Data

Bigan, Tammy.
    Nail art and design / Tammy Bigan
       p.   cm.
    Includes index.
    ISBN 1-56253-118-2
    1. Nail art (Manicuring)   I. Title
TT958.B54   1994
646.7'27–dc20   93-28383
                    CIP

SPECIAL THANK YOU:

Photography by
Steven Paul Knox

Thank you, Steven,
for your dedication.
God bless you.

•

Thank you, Mom, for
the inheritance of your
artistic talents.

SPECIAL NOTE FROM AUTHOR:

I hope that the information in
this book enriches the careers
of all the nail technicians who
read it and that their work
spreads smiles on the faces
of their customers.

Combine creativity and
imagination to develop your
own style of nail art!

Tammy Bigan

CONTENTS

FOREWORD

Incredible things are done to decorate fingernails, from simple polish to dazzling designs. Amazing art in tiny detail can leave anyone wondering how it was done, who did it, and with what. Designer nails are becoming more popular every day, and the need for more professionals to provide the service is growing.

In this book are detailed descriptions and instructions on many different types of nail designs, as well as lists of supplies and suggestions on where to get them.

Short or long, all nails at one time or another deserve some kind of special attention—a gold strip over red polish, a solid gold nail charm with a diamonds, or a freehand painting of a palm tree on a beach.

ACKNOWLEDGMENTS

I'd like to thank Clarice Sessanna, owner of Gals & Guys Beauty Salon of Pompano Beach, Florida, for the use of her nail art supplies. They were used to make all the nail designs in this book.

Step-By-Step Nail Art:
Tammy Bigan

Finished Nail Art Contributors:
Tammy Bigan
Brandy Kraft
Maria Miro
Michelle Valedon

Hand Models:
Tammy Bigan
Suzie Whalen
Lisa DeNeire

Snakes used for snake shots supplied by Kirk Norman

INTRODUCTION

Anything more than clear polish can be considered nail design. Yes, even one color of nail polish is a design. Its purpose is to make the client feel happy, to enhance the appearance of the nails, and to create a pleasing look. The same goes for designs that are not as simple.

What pleases some people may not please others. Individualism can be expressed with nail art. You can create hand-painted designs such as flowers or palm trees, or go even further and use decals, gemstones, or lace to decorate nails. Gold nails can even be glued on and worn as jewelry.

Many other things are used to design nail art, such as feathers, leather, or snakeskin. You can enhance interesting designs with silver or gold striping tape. Gold jewelry that is bolted on or hung as a dangling charm is designed for fingernails. Three-dimensional, or 3-D, nail art is shaped from acrylic to make fantasy come to life.

Nail art designs may go as far as the imagination can take them.

PART ONE

Supplies, Preservice Rules, and Beginning Steps

PART ONE
Supplies, Preservice Rules, and Beginning Steps

INTRODUCTION

Chapter 1 provides detailed
lists of materials, with
descriptions and uses, for
preparing and performing nail
design applications. Rules for
preservice sanitation and client
consultation are included in
chapter 2. Remember to
explain all the options
available and make sure your
clients understand design,
procedure, and cost before
you start to work on their nails.
It is important to remove
all existing nail polish from
the client's hands, and
to determine the physical
condition of the nails and
nail bed before proceeding.

•

The remaining chapters in
this part tell you how to
prepare the nails for the initial
base coat or background color
polish for the chosen design.

1 NAIL DESIGN SUPPLIES, DESCRIPTION, AND USAGE

Polishing Supplies

Orangewood Stick

This is a thin stick with flat ends that is used to remove polish from the cuticle. It is also used to apply gemstones and press nail tape down. You will find many uses for the orangewood stick; be sure you have several handy.

Base Coat

A base coat is applied under the colored enamel. It helps prevent stains on the nail bed from dark polish colors. It also helps protect the nail from drying and helps the polish wear longer.

Ridge Filler

Ridge filler can be used instead of a base coat. It is somewhat thicker than regular base coat and has a light, milky color. The thickness helps fill ridges and scratches on the nails to make a smooth foundation for the colored polish. In addition, ridge filler adds strength to soft or weak nails by making them thicker. It must dry completely before you apply polish.

Colored Nail Polish

The polish color should enhance the client's skin tone and overall appearance. Most clients will choose their own color but some may need suggestions. Application is one coat of base or ridge filler, two coats of color, and one or two coats of clear polish (top coat).

Some colored nail polishes are priced higher than others. To determine if they are worth it, try them out on a natural nail and watch how long they last and what condition the nail is in after the polish is removed. You should try this on the natural nail because acrylic and other nail wrap types hold polish longer so even the cheapest polish wears longer than expected.

Top Coat, or Clear Polish

Clear polish is used to shine natural nails or is applied over colored polish to seal and protect it. Clear polish is also used to adhere nail art to the nails and to cover completed nail designs.

Covering your work completely with clear polish keeps the design looking fresh. The polish should not be too thick in the bottle because most of the time several layers are required to bury a design and make the surface of the nail smooth.

Nail Design Supplies

There are so many design materials to choose from, to some the choice may be overwhelming. Others may find the combination of supplies delightful. (Fig. 1-1)

Figure 1-1   Combined nail art supplies

Nail Gems

Nail gems are available in many colors, shapes, and sizes. They are flat on one side and set easily into clear polish to make designs or add to a design. (Fig. 1-2)

Figure 1-2   Colorful nail gems

Nail Tape

This adhesive tape is available in several widths and many colors. (Fig. 1-3) Silver and gold are the most popular colors.

Figure 1-3   Red, black, and blue nail tape

Glitter

These tiny sparkles come in small packs or in little bottles. (Fig. 1-4) The bottles are easier to work with because you can squeeze the glitter out onto the nail in a particular spot. Glitter is available in many colors and can be used for creating a design or enhancing one.

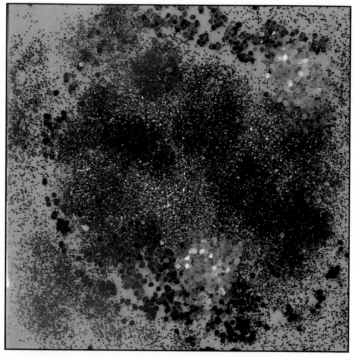

Figure 1-4   Glitter

Feathers

Beautiful feathers are used like decals. (Fig. 1-5) Combined with other art supplies, feathers can make interesting designs.

Figure 1-5   Feathers

Gold Leaf

Gold leaf can be applied to cover the nail, make a design over polish, or enhance another design. Silver, copper, or colored foil can also be used. (Fig. 1-6)

Figure 1-6   Gold and silver leaf

Bullion Beads

These are tiny glass beads that are coated in different colors (gold and silver seem to be the most popular). (Fig. 1-7) They are applied to the nail by using clear nail polish and can be used one by one or in clusters. They also make great additions to other nail art designs.

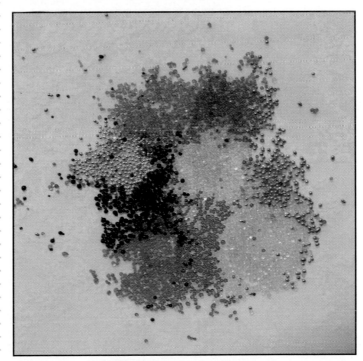

Figure 1-7   Bullion beads

Confetti

Confetti is small strips of foil that is available in many colors. It can be used to create a nail design or can be combined with other mediums. (Fig. 1-8)

Figure 1-8   Confetti

Lace

Lace can be used to cover an entire nail or part of a nail to create beautiful designs. (Fig. 1-9) Small lace patterns work best since the nail is small and you want the pattern to show. The thinner the lace is the easier it is to work with. Thick lace may be hard to adhere around the edges of the nail.

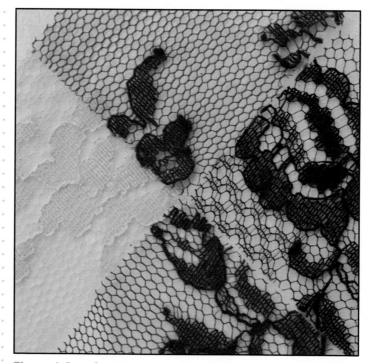

Figure 1-9   Lace

Pierced Nail Charm

Small charms are made for decorating fingernails. They are applied by drilling a hole in the nail with a hand drill and bolting the charm on with a tiny wrench that is at the other end of the drill. (Fig. 1-10)

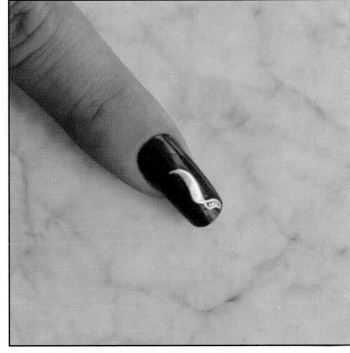

Figure 1-10   Pierced nail charm on colored polish

Gold Nails

Nails made of gold are custom fitted to the nail and adhered with glue. (Fig. 1-11)

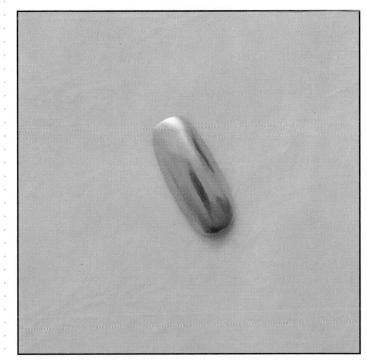

Figure 1-11   Gold nail

Leather and Snakeskin

Real leather and snakeskin can be used in strips to add to a design or completely cover the nail. It is unusual and always draws attention. (Fig. 1-12)

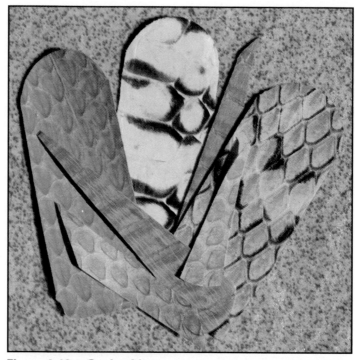

Figure 1-12   Snakeskins

Three-Dimensional, or 3-D, Nail Art

This is done by sculpting designs with acrylic to create a raised effect on the nail and then painting the design with paint or nail polish. The acrylic is formed over a reusable nail form, removed, filed, then glued to the nail. (Fig. 1-13)

Acrylic

The same acrylic that is used for acrylic nails is used for making nail art decorations.

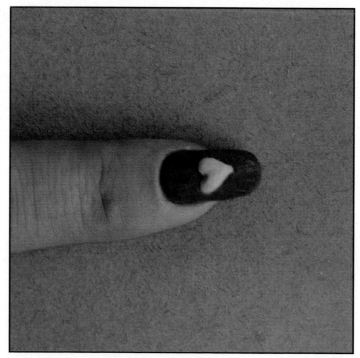

Figure 1-13   Heart-shaped 3-D nail art

Foil Art

Thin pieces of foil on plastic backing are adhered to the nail with a special emulsion glue. (Fig. 1-14) The plastic is pulled away after being pressed onto the dry glue, and the foil is left on the nail.

Emulsion Glue

This is a special glue used to adhere foil to a nail.

Figure 1-14   Foils

Nail Art Paint

Any kind of acrylic paint can be used to paint designs on the nails. (Fig. 1-15) Acrylic paints have a water base and are easy to use. You can make simple flowers or create a fantastic sea scene with the ocean and palm trees.

Figure 1-15   Acrylic paints

Nail Art Brushes

Small paint brushes available at art supply stores are used to paint tiny designs. You should have several sizes. (Fig. 1-16) Try a very skinny brush with long bristles to make thin stripes and a very small short-hair brush to make dots and to detail work. Try a small- or medium-size brush for painting backgrounds.

Note: Nail art supplies can be found at your local nail supply store. If distributors come to your salon, they should be able to find what you need. Suppliers you can order from always attend nail shows. Some supplies, like brushes and glitter, can be found at an arts and crafts store, where you may find other items with which you can decorate nails.

Wherever you find your supplies, remember that you are not limited to what is in this book (Fig. 1-17 shows one possible combination of supplies). Find new things, imagine, and create.

Figure 1-16   Small paint brushes

Figure 1-17   Paint design with gems, confetti, and glitter

2 PRESERVICE RULES

Exercise these preservice rules before performing any nail services on clients. Sanitation is the most important rule of every nail service, and it must be followed constantly.

1. Follow all sanitation and sterilization rules. Wash your hands and have clients wash their hands with antiseptic soap.

2. Before removing nail polish ask clients if they are wearing nail tips or any type of wrap. If so, use nonacetone polish remover instead of the regular type. Regular polish remover or acetone will damage the tips and wraps.

3. Check for any possible nail disorders. If any contagious disorder is found, consult client for care and treatment and schedule a new appointment.

4. Sanitize all nail beds.

5. Consult with client about needed service.

6. While doing nails, make client aware of home care procedures.

7. Explain the possibility of mold or fungus if nails are improperly maintained or neglected.

3 WHERE TO START

Always start on a clean nail bed. Whether it is a tip and wrap or just the natural nail, it must be clean. Have clients wash their hands with antiseptic soap. If necessary, give a manicure or gently push back cuticles. Making your design on a clean, strong nail will enhance your work and help it last longer.

1. Remove all nail polish and polish residue from nails. Clean nail grooves and cuticles gently and thoroughly (see removing polish).

2. Use nail antiseptic to sanitize nail beds and let dry.

3. Consult with client about the desired design. Try to suggest several designs from which to choose. Have sample designs ready on a chart or some type of display.

4. After design is selected, lay out on your table the supplies required for that particular design.

5. Protect your terry towel with a disposable drop cloth.

6. To avoid any misunderstanding, discuss the charge for the design chosen before starting.

Points to Remember

• Suggest designs that match the client's personality.

• Nails and cuticles must be in good condition to enhance design and to help it last as long as possible.

• Tell client how to care for design.

• Keep the length of nail in mind when choosing a design.

4 REMOVING EXISTING NAIL POLISH

Before any nail service can be given, polish must be removed and/or nail surface cleaned. A cotton ball or sterile pad is saturated with polish remover and rubbed over the nail to clean it. Be sure nails are completely free from old polish and residue.

Supplies Needed

Nail polish remover, nonacetone or regular

Cotton or sterile pads

Orangewood stick or polish correcting tool of choice

Paper towels

Procedure

1. If using cotton, roll into tight ball.

2. Hold the ball between your first finger and thumb, squeeze top of ball while saturating the bottom with polish remover. If you want to protect your own polish hold ball with lower part of finger and thumb instead of fingertips.

3. Squeeze heavy drip off bottom of ball and continue to squeeze top of ball. By squeezing the top you are keeping the polish remover at the bottom of ball where it is needed.

4. Press ball on base of nail bed and move from side to side while sliding down nail. Do not make big movements with the ball of remover or you will spread what is coming off all over cuticles and end of finger.

5. If polish is thick, you can repeat several times with new balls of cotton and remover. When ball of cotton is full of dissolved polish, throw it out and make a new one.

6. Use an orangewood stick to remove polish from cuticle or nail groove.

7. Sanitize all nails and let dry.

Points to Remember

• Follow preservice rules.

• Ask clients if they are wearing tips or wraps before removing polish.

• Clean all the polish from nails and cuticles.

• If you hold pad or cotton ball with the underside of your knuckles and squeeze, the remover won't disturb your polish.

5 POLISHING NAILS— STANDARD PROCEDURE

The first thing you must do to prepare for most nail art is polish the nails. This creates a backdrop for your work. Apply the base coat then two layers of color, which must dry in between layers, and finish with a coat of clear polish (top coat). The top coat is very important; without it, or if it is not dry before you begin, the polish color will bleed through your design making it look murky and messy.

A perfect polish job is as close to the cuticle as possible without touching it. Each layer should be even and not too thick, and there should be no lumps or streaks when finished. If polish is applied too thick or if the layers are applied too close together, the polish will stay tacky and take forever to dry completely resulting in smudged nail polish.

When designing on nails that are weak or have ridges, if the client does not want the nails wrapped a ridge filler can replace the base coat. This will help make the polish and design last longer and add body to the nails to give them more strength.

Supplies Needed

Base coat or ridge filler

Desired nail polish color

Clear polish

Orangewood stick or polish correcting stick

Procedure

1. Extend pinky finger of hand holding the brush and use it to brace your hand by placing it on the table, your other hand, or a comfortable resting place.

2. Hold client's finger from underneath and gently pull cuticle away from nail bed. Hold cuticle like this when polishing to keep polish off it.

3. Dip brush into bottle of base coat and wipe it on the inside of the bottle to remove excess polish. If nails are long, leave more polish on the brush; if nails are short, leave less polish on the brush.

4. Cover nail evenly with the polish. The more pressure you use on the brush, the more polish you spread on the nail.

5. To get close to the moon, place wet brush near the cuticle and press base of brush down to make bristles spread apart making an arc. Jiggle brush while pushing up toward cuticle. Having the bristles spread out helps push the polish up in an arched shape. Pull brush down nail. Finish painting the nail by covering the sides.

6. Let base coat dry.

7. Apply first coat of color using same technique. Let dry for a moment.

8. Apply second coat of color. Be sure sides are covered and there is a clean line at the moon where polish and cuticle meet.

9. Use orangewood stick to remove any unwanted polish from cuticles.

10. Cover with clear polish and let nails dry for ten minutes before starting nail designs.

Points to Remember

- Do not use ridge filler if several extra layers of polish are going to be used to complete a design or it will be too thick and will never dry completely.

- Let each coat dry between application to ensure proper drying.

- Use polish brush to your advantage by manipulating it with pressure to control the spread of the bristles and application of the polish.

- Clean mistakes on cuticle with orangewood stick.

- When polishing very long nails you can paint the free edge first then the rest of nail.

- Cover color with clear polish and let dry before continuing with design or color will bleed through and damage design.

Helpful hint:

When removing excess polish from cuticle and nail groove try placing orangewood stick on the edge of cuticle instead of the nail groove. Gently rotate the tool to pull cuticle away from nail just a little. While holding cuticle back carefully wipe area.

PART TWO

Creating Nail Designs

PART TWO
Creating Nail Designs

INTRODUCTION

Nail art designs range from simple, single-color nail applications to elaborate combinations of colors, gems, feathers, 3-D scenes, and more. The following sixteen chapters take you step-by-step through art and design applications. The nail design materials defined in Part 1 are described in more detail. You'll find specific procedures and additional points to remember for each type of application.

•

You start out easy with layering colors; move steadily through all the individual nail design supplies like gems, beads, and feathers; then move on to the more challenging snakeskin, leather, 3-D, and freehand art designs.

•

Once you are familiar with each technique, you'll have endless combinations of designs to choose from and to keep your clients dazzled and dazzling!

6 FRENCH MANICURE

The French manicure, also known as the white-tip manicure, is a special way of polishing the nails so they look natural, with white tips, and appear to be all the same length even if they are not. After the tips are painted white the nails are covered with sheer beige or sheer pink. (Fig. 6-1)

Some variations of the French manicure have become very popular. Some are made with a V shape or straight across for a boxy look. (Fig. 6-2)

Supplies Needed

Complete French manicure kit or base coat, beige or pink natural tone, white color, clear polish

Orangewood stick

Procedure

Remember to brace your hand with extended pinky to help avoid shaking.

1. Prepare nails.

2. Apply base coat and let dry.

Figure 6-1 The elegant, simple look of a French manicure

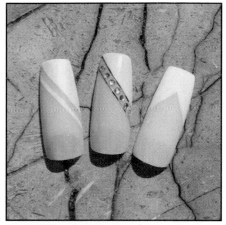

Figure 6-2 French manicure variations

3. Shake bottle of white very well before using. It gets thick quicker than most colors and needs to be shaken about every other nail if it seems sticky. If polish gets too thick thin it out or discard it. Thick white will not dry quickly enough and the design will get smudged.

4. Hold client's finger from underneath and have client relax completely so you can turn finger easily. To paint nail turn client's finger in one direction and the white strip in the other direction. Make one clean swipe from one side of free edge to the other. Repeat in same manner on other side. The strip should cover the free edge to where the nail bed starts. If a nail is shorter than the others you can paint the strip lower to make the strips even.

This step is important to assure the design looks its best. Let the white strip dry completely before continuing. If a second coat is desired for a whiter effect you must let both coats dry between layers or the polish can remain tacky or never dry completely. Paint all ten tips then proceed.

5. Apply the polish of choice, completely covering the nail. Let dry a couple of minutes and apply a second coat if needed.

6. Apply the clear polish to protect design. You can dress up the design by applying an opalescent or silver-white before the clear. A quick dry can be used if desired.

Points to Remember

- Keep a steady hand by bracing yourself with extended pinky.

- Do not make white strip thick or it will not dry properly.

- Make the width of the white the same on each nail to make all nails look the same length.

- Let every layer of polish dry between coats. It is better to take a little extra time to do it right than having to do it over or fix it.

- For fun, try making the white tip a different shape, or use a different sheer color on the top.

7 LAYERED NAIL POLISH DESIGNS

By layering the polish colors you can create beautiful designs such as stripes, V shapes, and multicolored swirls. By layering the different colors while making a different line of design on each layer you create layered polish designs. (Fig. 7-1)

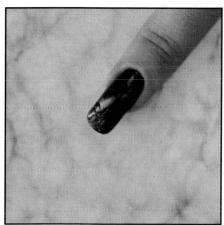

Figure 7-1 A nail designed with multicolored, layered polish

Supplies Needed

Several colors of nail polish that match or complement each other

Orangewood stick

Polish remover

Procedure

1. Apply base coat and let dry.

2. Apply one coat of colored polish that you want to be the base color, meaning the color at the bottom of the design.

3. Apply second coat of base color to base of nail, making it thinner at the free edge. (You want it thinner because you are going to be layering the polish over the free edge several times, and if it builds up or gets too thick it will never dry.) Let dry.

4. After the base layers are dry use a second color to paint the end of the nail at an angle leaving a space at the base of nail so the base color is showing. (Fig. 7-2)

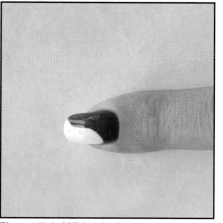

Figure 7-2 White is the second color of this layered design.

Note: You can stop here or layer several more times using another color or switching the two colors. (Figs. 7-3, 7-4) Let each layer dry between applications. Use your imagination to create swirl patterns or hard-edged designs. (Figs. 7-5–7-7)

5. After pattern is complete and has dried, protect and seal it with clear polish.

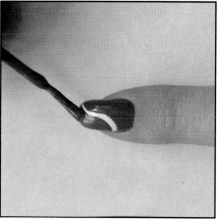

Figure 7-3 Applying base color over white for layered design

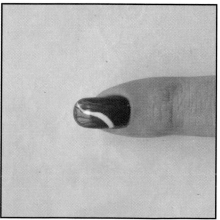

Figure 7-4 Layered design after top coat is applied

Figure 7-5 Layered design with three colors

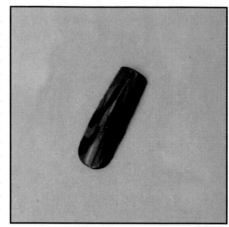

Figure 7-6 Black and blue layered design

Points to Remember

• Let each layer dry between applications.

• Make the polish thinner at the free edge so polish is not too thick when design at the end of nail is complete.

• Cover design with clear polish to seal.

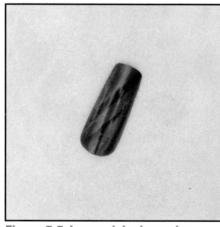

Figure 7-7 Layered design using straight lines

8

GEMSTONE APPLICATION

Nails can be beautifully enhanced with gemstones or rhinestones. The gem or gems are placed on the nail into wet clear polish. When the polish is dry the gem is stuck to the nail. You can also combine the gems with other art mediums to create intriguing designs.

Supplies Needed

Clear polish

Orangewood stick

Nail gemstones or rhinestones

Preparation

Polish nails in regular manner. Do not forget the top coat. If designing over other art mediums, complete them first and let dry then garnish with the gems.

Procedure

1. Determine where you want to place the gem or gems.

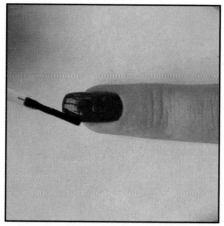

Figure 8-1 Apply clear dots for gem placement.

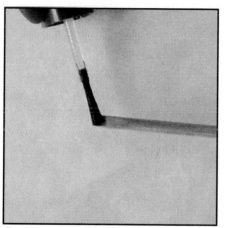

Figure 8-2 Apply clear polish to orangewood stick.

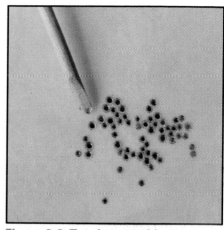

Figure 8-3 Touch gem with wet end of stick.

Figure 8-4 Apply and press gem to nail.

2. Place one drop of clear polish on nail where you want the gem to be. (Fig. 8-1)

3. Apply a small amount of clear polish to end of an orangewood stick. (Fig. 8-2)

4. Touch wet end of stick to the top of a gem. (Fig. 8-3)

5. Press gem onto dot of polish on nail. (Fig. 8-4)

6. Repeat steps one through five until design is complete.

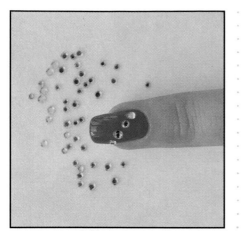

Figure 8-5 Nail gems after top coat
is applied

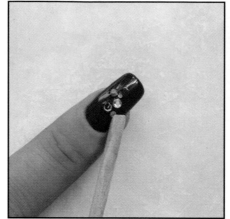

Figure 8-6 In-progress multicolored
gem design

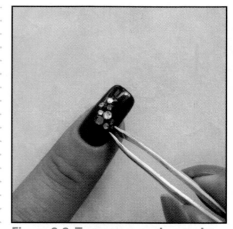

Figure 8-8 Tweezers can be used
instead of the
orangewood stick.

7. After gems are in place apply
one layer of clear polish over
entire design and let dry.
(Fig. 8-5) Do not apply too
quickly or air bubbles
can appear.

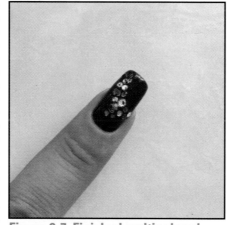

Figure 8-7 Finished multicolored
gem design

The same procedure is used for
multicolored and different sized
gems. (Figs. 8-6, 8-7) You can
use tweezers instead of the
orangewood stick to apply the
gems. Use the brush to apply
clear drops on the nail for
placement. Then use the tweezer
to pick up, place, and press the
gem on the nail. (Fig. 8-8)

Points To Remember

• Always apply a top coat and let
it dry before starting design to
avoid disturbing the polish or
base design.

• Set gems in wet drops or spots
of clear polish.

• You can adjust the position of
gems by carefully pushing them
with an orangewood stick.

• When applying top coat, brush
it on gently and slowly to avoid
air bubbles.

9

NAIL TAPE APPLICATION

Nails are decorated with thin tape that is available in many colors and widths. Gold and silver are among the favorite colors. The tape is used alone or combined with other nail design supplies.

After the design is completed a coat of clear polish is applied to seal it on the nail.

Supplies Needed

Self-adhesive nail tape

Clear polish

Sharp nippers or small sharp scissors

Preparation

Polish nails in regular manner. Apply top coat and let dry completely. (Fig. 9-1) If applying nail tape over another design, the design must be dry.

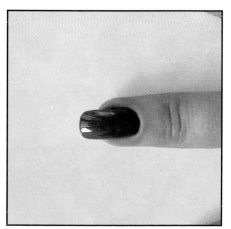

Figure 9-1 A dry nail ready for tape

Procedure

You can have a pattern in mind when you start or use your imagination to create an original design every time.

1. Hold the end of tape in one hand and hold the roll of tape, sticky side down, in the other.

2. Place tape on the nail in desired spot and cut the tape off at end of roll (leave the ends long until pattern is complete).

3. Use orangewood stick to firmly press tape into place. Be sure there are no air bubbles under tape and that ends are well pressed down.

4. Continue applying tape to complete design, leaving the ends hanging over the free edge and cuticles. (Fig. 9-2)

5. Trim all tape ends with nippers or scissors. Trimming all the ends at the same time assures the tape will meet evenly. (Fig. 9-3)

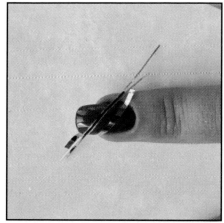

Figure 9-2 Tape in place with ends extending beyond nail

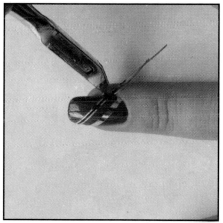

Figure 9-3 Trimming the tape ends with nippers

6. Check to see that all tape ends are pressed down and stuck to nail. If ends won't stay down, you can apply a small amount of clear polish under them, let it dry a little, then press ends down with an orangewood stick. (Fig. 9-4)

7. Apply clear polish over nail, covering tape and edges of nail completely. (Fig. 9-5)

8. Let dry and check tape ends to be sure they are secure. If they are not, gently press with an orangewood stick until they stay down. Apply another layer of clear polish to secure tape ends. (Fig. 9-6)

Points to Remember

• Be sure top coat is completely dry before applying tape.

• Trim all ends at the same time to make them even.

• Do not touch back of tape or it will not be sticky enough.

• Put a small drop of clear polish under the ends if they stick up, let dry a little, then press again.

• To avoid making bubbles that might distort or clutter your design, do not apply top coat too quickly.

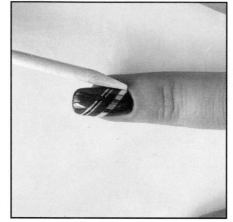

Figure 9-4 Press tape ends down with orangewood stick.

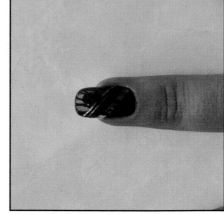

Figure 9-6 Finished tape design

Figure 9-5 Apply clear polish on nail and tape.

10 GLITTER ART

Glitter can be applied to the nails over clear or colored polish. It is easy and fun and designs can be simple or elaborate. You can cover the whole nail, just the tip, or a dot in the middle—your imagination rules.

Supplies Needed

Large piece of paper

Clear polish

Glitter in desired color or colors

Preparation

If colored base coat is desired, apply colored polish and let dry completely.

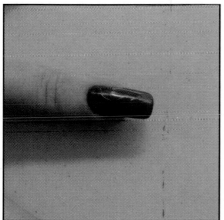

Figure 10-1 Apply clear polish where you want glitter.

Procedure

1. Place large piece of paper under hand on table to catch extra falling glitter.

2. Apply clear polish to nail in area you want to cover with glitter. All other areas of nail must be completely dry before applying glitter. The glitter will stick to all wet or damp areas. (Fig. 10-1)

3. Before the clear polish dries sprinkle the glitter over it, covering it completely. (Fig. 10-2)

4. Gently tap the finger to shake glitter off the rest of the nail. A small duster brush can be used, but remember your sanitation rules and clean the brush between clients. Do not blow on the nail, as that is also unsanitary.

5. Let this section dry. Apply more clear polish to another part of nail if you want to use another glitter color, and complete steps three and four. (Fig. 10-3)

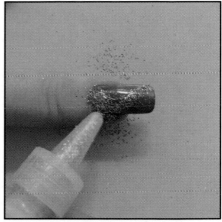

Figure 10-2 Sprinkle glitter over clear polish.

Figure 10-3 Add the second glitter color.

Figure 10-4 **Finished glitter design after two layers of clear polish**

6. When design is complete, cover with two layers of clear polish to seal glitter. (Fig. 10-4)

Points to Remember

- Glitter sticks to wet or damp surfaces so be sure the nail is dry except where you want the glitter to stick.

- Gently remove extra glitter from nail or you could destroy the design and have to start over.

- Seal glitter design with at least two layers of clear polish to be sure it is covered completely and won't rub off.

11 FEATHER ART

Feathers, alone or combined with other art mediums, make great designs on nails. Nail art designs using feathers are some of the most beautiful and admired. Following are the basic rules for application of a feather to a nail. You may use your imagination and create your own designs by using this technique.

The feather is applied to the nail using clear nail polish under and over the feather to inlay it into the polish. You may cover the whole nail or just part of it.

Supplies Needed

Clear polish

Feathers

Small scissors

Orangewood stick

Tweezers

Preparation

Polish nails in regular manner and let dry.

Procedure

1. Choose feather to be used and clean any excess fur from the end of its stem.

2. Apply clear polish to nail.

3. Hold stem of feather with tweezers or fingertip, whichever is easier. Set side of feather onto wet polish. (Fig. 11-1)

4. If you need to adjust the feather, you can pull down on stem to move it down the nail. Use orangewood stick to press feather flat onto nail. (Fig. 11-2)

5. Apply clear polish in direction of feather strings so they do not pop up.

6. Let dry. While it is drying you can gently push feather into polish to smooth out.

Figure 11-1 Set feather onto wet clear polish.

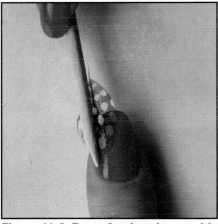

Figure 11-2 Press feather down with orangewood stick.

Figure 11-3 Trim edges as close to nail as possible.

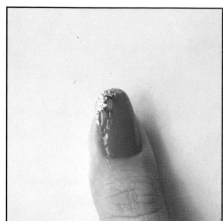

Figure 11-5 Feather design with gold leaf

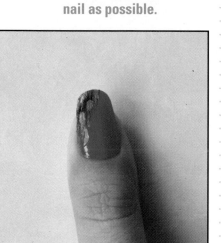

Figure 11-4 Apply clear polish to seal feather in place.

Figure 11-6 Fancy feather design with gold leaf and bullion beads.

7. Trim edges of feather using sharp scissors. Trim as close as possible so feather doesn't hang from nail edge and catch on things. (Fig. 11-3)

8. Apply second coat of clear polish, completely covering nail and feather. Pay attention to the feather edges.

9. A second or third coat of clear polish can be applied to completely seal feather into polish. Let each coat dry between layers. (Fig. 11-4)

Once you feel confident applying feathers, try your hand at adding other materials to your designs. (Figs. 11-5, 11-6)

Points to Remember

- Be sure colored polish and top coat are dry before you apply the clear polish into which you set feather.

- Trim feather close to edges of nail.

- Apply the clear polish slowly to avoid air bubbles.

- Several coats of clear polish can be used to seal feather in polish.

12 GOLD LEAF APPLICATION

This is an elegant and beautiful way of decorating nails; even the very conservative client will go for it. The gold and silver leaf is very delicate and light. It blows away easily so you have to be careful not to breathe hard when working with it. Keeping your tools clean while working with gold leaf makes controlling it a lot easier.

A little speck on the corner of the nail suits some people. Others might like it over a feather and garnished with a gemstone. No matter what design is desired, this is a very popular medium.

Supplies Needed

Clear polish

Gold or silver leaf

Orangewood stick

Tweezers

Preparation

Complete design or polish desired. Cover with clear polish and let dry.

Procedure

1. Apply clear nail polish on area you want covered with gold. (Fig. 12-1)

2. Using tweezers and orangewood stick, place bits of gold on nail and gently press into wet polish. (Fig. 12-2) Continue doing this until design is complete. (Fig. 12-3)

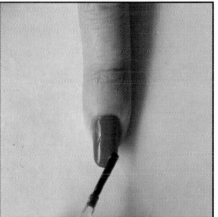

Figure 12-1 Apply clear polish to area of nail on which you want gold leaf to adhere.

Figure 12-2 Apply gold leaf to wet polish.

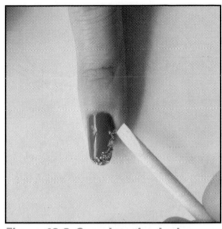

Figure 12-3 Complete the design.

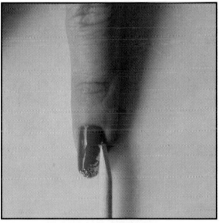

Figure 12-4 Press gold leaf flat on nail.

3. Use orangewood stick to press gold leaf flat on nail. (Fig. 12-4)

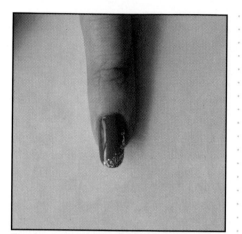

Figure 12-5 Apply clear polish over gold leaf to seal design.

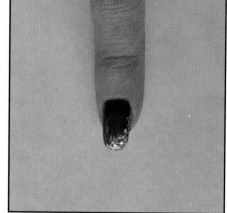

Figure 12-6 Gold leaf with gems

Points to Remember

• Keep tweezers and orangewood stick clean so gold does not build up on tools.

• Apply the clear polish slowly to avoid air bubbles.

• Let base design dry well before starting or the gold will sink into the color and look messy.

4. Apply clear polish over gold leaf to seal. Let dry. (Fig. 12-5) If you are going to add striping tape or a gemstone, do it before applying the final coat of clear polish. (Fig. 12-6)

5. A second or third coat of clear polish may be applied if needed to cover nail design. Let each layer dry slightly before applying the next.

13 BULLION BEADS

Bullion beads are used to create or enhance nail designs. The beads are available in many colors, but the gold and silver beads are the most popular. You can cover the nail entirely or partially, or apply the beads one by one.

Supplies Needed

Bullion beads in desired colors

Clear polish

Orangewood stick

Preparation

Paint nail or nails with desired color and one layer of top coat. Let dry five minutes.

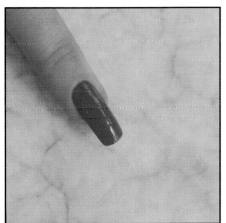

Figure 13-1 Apply clear polish to nail for bullion bead placement.

Procedure

1. Apply clear polish on nail in the area you want the beads. (Fig. 13-1)

2. Dip nail upside down into the beads, and the beads will stick into the clear polish. Arrange the edges of design with orangewood stick. (Fig. 13-2)

Figure 13-2 Arrange edge of beads with orangewood stick.

If covering a small area you can apply the beads with an orangewood stick the same way you apply gemstones.

3. Apply clear polish to another area of nail and dip again.

4. Continue the coating and dipping process until design is complete. (Fig. 13-3)

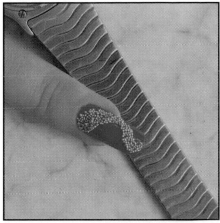

Figure 13-3 Completed one-color bullion bead design.

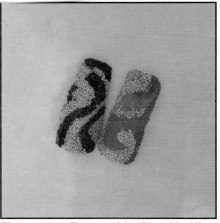

Figure 13-4 Two multicolored bullion bead designs

5. Cover design with two layers of clear polish to secure.

Cover the edge of the nail with beads, create a strip of beads in the middle, or use your own design. To make a detailed pattern you can use an orangewood stick to apply the beads in the same manner as gemstones. (Fig. 13-4)

Points to Remember

• Let the first layer of top coat over the color dry before making design or the color will bleed through.

• Arrange the beads with orangewood stick after each color so design is neat.

• Seal the design with at least two coats of clear polish to adhere it to the nail.

14 LACE DESIGNS

Lace makes an excellent accessory to an evening gown and is a fun addition when wearing blue jeans. It is applied on colored polish with clear polish acting as the adhesive. You can cover part or all of the nail and use other art mediums to add to the design. Use thin or fine lace with tiny patterns to get the most out of your lace designs.

Supplies Needed

Lace or net fabric

Clear polish

Orangewood stick

Small scissors

Preparation

Polish nails with desired color and one layer of top coat. Let dry.

Procedure

1. Cut section of lace to fit over nail or part of nail.

2. Apply clear polish over area where lace is to be placed and let dry a little (until it is sticky).

3. Place lace over the clear polish and press into place with an orangewood stick. (Fig. 14-1) Do not press lace too hard or you could push it into the color below making it look messy.

4. After lace is pressed into place trim all edges so they do not hang over the nail edges or onto cuticle. (Fig. 14-2)

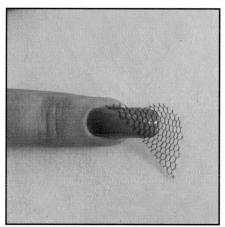

Figure 14-1 Place lace on wet nail.

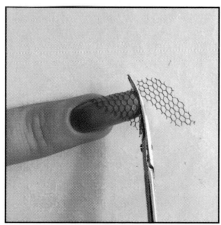

Figure 14-2 Trim lace edges close to nail.

5. Apply clear polish to seal. (Fig. 14-3) Several layers of clear polish should be used to completely lacquer the lace so that the surface is smooth to touch when dry. Let every layer dry between applications.

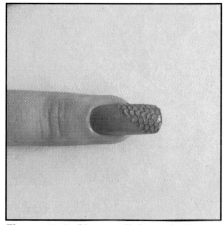

Figure 14-3 Clear polish seals the lace onto the nail.

Note: To further enhance the design, nail tape, bullion beads, and/or gemstones can be added before the final layers of clear polish are applied (Figs. 14-4, 14-5.)

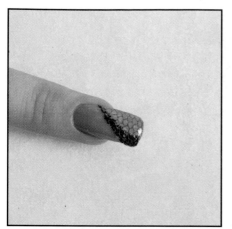

Figure 14-4 Lace with black bullion bead design

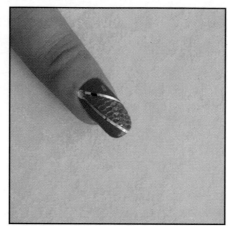

Figure 14-5 Lace with silver tape and gem design

Points to Remember

• Let clear polish dry just a little so it is sticky. This makes the lace stick better.

• Trim all edges evenly so there is no lace hanging over the nail edges to get snagged on things.

• Cover with clear polish until lace is buried. Let each coat dry in between.

15 PIERCED NAIL CHARM

Pierced is the key word here. Yes, a hole is drilled through the free edge of the nail with a tiny hand drill. Then a gold charm is screwed in and bolted in the back.

There are many designs from which to choose. Usually they are real gold, but some are available in gold plate. They come plain or with diamonds or other jewels on them. The pierced nail charm is a great retail item for you to carry.

The charms can be applied to the natural nail, but a wrapped nail is much stronger. Clients should be advised to wrap the nail wearing the charm.

Supplies Needed

Clear polish

Nail charm

Hand drill for charm

Tweezers

Note: Make sure the company that supplies your charm also supplies the right size drill for the charm. (Fig. 15-1) Some companies have different type drills and wrenches so you should follow the instructions supplied by the company.

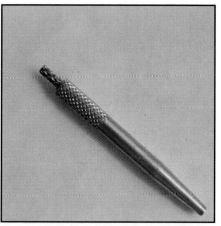

Figure 15-1 Hand drill for nail charm

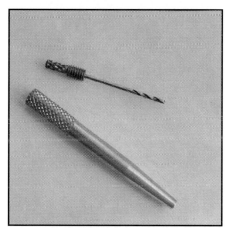

Figure 15-2 Remove drill bit from handle.

Preparing the hand drill

The drill bit is stored in the sheathlike drill handle. Remove the bit. (Fig. 15-2) With drill bit facing out, screw the bit back on the handle and tighten. (Fig. 15-3) On the other end of the drill is a wrench hole with which to screw the bolt on. (Fig. 15-4)

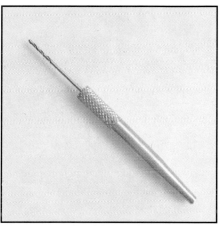

Figure 15-3 Put bit into handle with drill facing out and tighten.

Figure 15-4 Bolt in wrench

Preparation

Paint nail and let dry completely or drill hole first and then paint nail. Whichever way you choose, the charm must be applied to the nail after it has been polished. The polish must be dry.

Procedure

1. Choose the location for the charm. It must go on the free edge not too close to the nail bed. If you try to put it too close to the nail bed, you might hit the underside of the finger and it will be difficult to get the bolt on the back. If you put it too close to the end of the free edge, the extra weight can weaken the nail and make it break easier.

2. Support the free edge with your finger or by placing it firmly on the table. Place drill bit on the nail where you want the charm and twist drill clockwise while pressing down. Keep twisting and pressing until the drill bit makes a hole in the free edge. (Figs. 15-5–15-7)

   If this is difficult you can try turning the client's hand upside down and drilling from the back. This method supports the nail better, but it is harder to judge exactly where the hole will be. Double check to be sure you are drilling in the right spot.

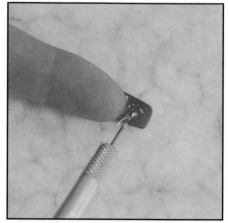

Figure 15-5 Twist drill to make hole.

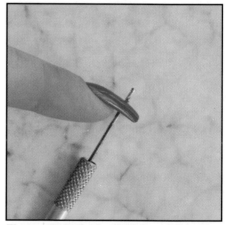

Figure 15-6 Twist drill through nail.

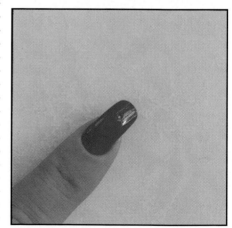

Figure 15-7 Hole in free edge of nail

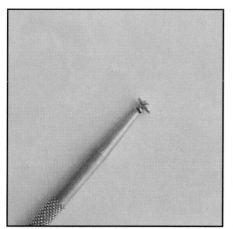

Figure 15-8 Use wrench to remove bolt from charm.

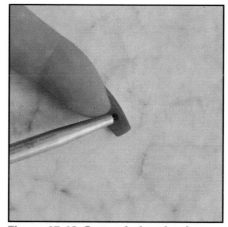

Figure 15-10 Screw bolt to back of charm.

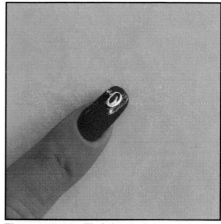

Figure 15-12 Finished pierced nail charm on nail

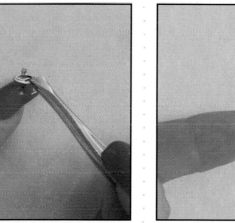

Figure 15-9 Use tweezers to place charm in hole.

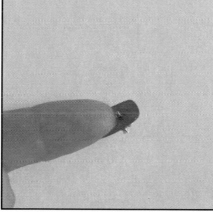

Figure 15-11 Apply clear polish to back of nail, covering bolt.

3. Dust area and use wrench end of drill to remove bolt from back of charm. (Fig. 15-8)

4. Hold charm with tweezers, place it into the hole, and turn it to the desired position. (Fig. 15-9)

5. Using wrench end of the drill, place the bolt on the screw on back of nail. Using the wrench turn the bolt clockwise to tighten. (Fig. 15-10) Do not overtighten the bolt.

6. Look at charm to see that it is still in desired position. If it has turned, then reposition it and hold it with your finger while you tighten the bolt a little more.

7. Once the charm is in position and the bolt is tight, apply clear polish to the back of nail covering the bolt so it cannot twist off. (Fig. 15-11)

8. Clear polish may also be used over the top of the completed charm design to keep it from catching in hair or snagging clothes. (Fig. 15-12)

9. Most charm companies sell a screw cutter to trim extra length off the screw. If the screw is too long, cut it off a little above the bolt. Do not cut it too short because you might eventually want to move the charm to another thicker nail. If cut too short, it will not fit.

Points to Remember

- Choose a location for charm that will not stress the nail or make it break.

- Drill hole straight or charm will not lay flat on nail.

- Be sure polish is dry before applying charm.

- Put clear polish on back of charm to keep bolt from turning. Cover top of charm if required.

- Trim off back of screw if it is sticking out excessively.

Maintaining charm

After a week or so a polish change will be needed. Hold cotton with remover on the back of nail to loosen polish around the bolt. After it is loose, use the wrench to remove bolt. Remove any polish on the top of the charm. After top is clean remove the charm, change the polish, and let dry. Apply charm in same hole using same method.

Moving Charm

After the nail grows for several weeks the charm may need to be moved to a different spot or even another nail. In either case, the existing hole will need to be filled and a new one made.

To fill the hole, wrap the area with same type of wrap that is already on nail, and cover the back of the hole with glue. If there is no wrap on the nail, you may put a little cotton through the hole and glue it. Nip the extra cotton off both sides of nail and buff smooth. Do not remove dust. Apply more glue and spread it evenly to smooth both sides. Let glue dry and buff nail on top and underneath (to reach underneath, use a folded disk buffer or an electric drill with a buffer on it).

Points to Remember

- Fill hole on both sides or it will have a weak spot that might break or crack.

- Be sure back of nail is buffed smooth so it does not catch on things or collect dirt.

16 GOLD NAIL APPLICATION

Gold nails are glued on the nail bed and worn as jewelry. They are beautiful if applied and fit properly. Gold nails are available in many different styles. Some have diamonds or birthstones on them, and others are plain or engraved. (Fig. 16-1)

It is important that you use the right size nail. The gold nail should be wide enough to cover the nail but not so wide that it hangs over the side onto the cuticle. If gold nails are more than twice the length of the wearer's nail bed, they tend to fall off.

When purchased for retail gold nails should come with a sizing kit and instructions for application. The adhesive should come with the kit, but if it is not included you can use contact glue.

The following instructions explain how a gold nail is fitted and applied.

Supplies Needed

Gold nail that is the same width as the nail bed

Contact glue or double-sided tape

Hard file

Orangewood stick

Figure 16-1 Gold nail

Procedure

1. Clean nail bed. Be sure there is no polish residue on nail bed.

2. File natural nail oval and short so it does not show from the sides or under the gold nail. A little nail can show under the gold nail, but less is better.

Note: If it will fit properly, a gold nail can be applied over wrapped nails as long as they are not too thick.

3. Lightly roughen top of nail bed with file for better adhesion. Dust nail.

4. Size gold nail so it fits the nail bed perfectly. If you are unable to find the right size, use one slightly larger and file the sides a little at a time with a heavy file. Be careful not to overfile and make the nail too small.

5. Apply adhesive to fingernail. Let it dry for a minute.

6. Apply adhesive to the base of gold nail filling the area that will be on the fingernail. Let dry.

7. Press gold nail onto fingernail and hold for twenty seconds. The gold nail should adhere to the fingernail.

8. If any glue squeezes out onto cuticle, wipe it off with an orangewood stick.

9. Tell client the glue needs to set and dry for twenty minutes before normal use of finger.

Tape-On Method

The same procedure is used with double-sided tape as with glue, but you put the tape on the fingernail and then place the gold nail over it. It is difficult to adjust the gold nail once it is pressed down so be sure the gold nail is in the right position before pressing it down onto tape.

Points to Remember

- Clean and roughen fingernail then remove dust.

- Press firmly but not so hard that the glue squeezes out from the sides or there won't be enough to hold nail in place.

- Clean excess glue from cuticle with an orangewood stick.

- If using double-sided tape, put tape on nail bed not the gold nail. This ensures the nail bed is completely covered with tape.

- Do not overfile gold nail when sizing it.

Removing Gold Nail

After ten days to two weeks the nail should be removed and reapplied in the proper place. The natural nail is constantly growing forward and, as the gold nail is attached, it will also move forward, leaving a gap between the gold nail and the cuticle. This looks ugly and can damage the natural nail.

Procedure for Gold Nail Removal

1. Soak finger in required glue solvent. (The type of glue being used will determine the type of solvent required.)

2. Use orangewood stick to gently lift gold nail off natural nail. If it does not lift away easily, soak nail a few more minutes and try again. Do not force the gold nail off if it is not loose or you can tear the natural nail.

3. Wipe the remaining glue off natural nail and buff with soft buffer.

4. Reapply gold nail in proper place or give other desired service.

Gold Nail Precautions

Air, moisture, and bacteria can get caught between the gold nail and the natural nail. This can cause a fungus to grow on the natural nail. To avoid this, the finger with the gold nail can be dipped in alcohol.

All clients should be made aware of this possibility. If the nail is properly applied and maintained a fungus should not grow, but you do not know for sure what clients are doing to or with their hands and fingers after they leave your table and it is better to be safe than sorry.

Do not use fast-drying glues to apply the gold nail. This glue becomes brittle and will not hold the nail on properly. If the nail is banged or hit, the glue can separate from the gold nail and the nail can fall off. Use only the glue recommended by the gold nail supplier.

17 SNAKESKIN AND LEATHER DESIGNS

Incredible as it may sound, it's true. Real leather and snakeskin can be applied to the nail in decorative strips or to completely cover the nail. To achieve the best look, the leather used should be thin. Strips can be cut into a V shape or an S shape, or any other pattern you can think of, and then applied to the nail over polish to make or complete a design.

Use contact glue or clear nail polish as an adhesive. You can cover the snakeskin and leather with clear polish so they won't get wet. The clear polish will darken the color of the leather or snakeskin.

You can purchase snakeskin and leather at supply stores or arts and craft stores.

Supplies Needed

Snakeskin or leather

Clear polish

Tweezers

Small scissors

Orangewood stick

Preparation

Polish nails. Apply one coat of clear polish and let it dry completely.

Procedure

1. Cut strips of leather or snakeskin to desired shape.

2. Apply clear polish on nail where the strip is to be placed. Do not use too much or it will bleed out from under the strip. Use tweezers to pick up and place snakeskin or leather on nail. (Fig. 17-1)

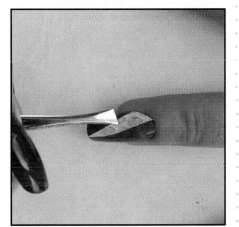

Figure 17-1 Place snakeskin on wet nail with tweezers.

3. Press strip onto nail and smooth with orangewood stick. (Fig. 17-2)

4. Trim excess with scissors so that it does not hang over the edge of the nail or touch the cuticle. (Fig. 17-3)

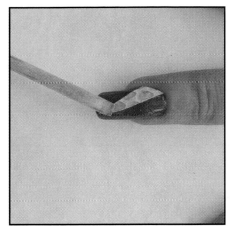

Figure 17-2 Press snakeskin flat onto nail with orangewood stick.

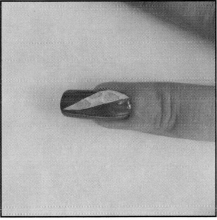

Figure 17-3 Snakeskin is trimmed and flat and smooth on nail.

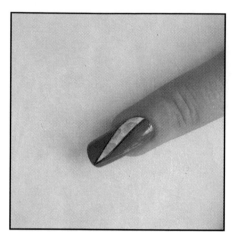

Figure 17-4 Snakeskin design rimmed with black tape

Figure 17-5 Snakeskin with tape strips design against snakeskin background

5. Trim design with striping tape, nail gems, or any other decoration you think will enhance it. (Figs. 17-4, 17-5)

6. Cover entire nail with two or three coats of clear polish, letting each layer dry between application.

Covering Entire Nail with Leather or Snakeskin

Use same supplies as with strip application.

Procedure

1. Cut piece of snakeskin or leather to approximate size of nail to be covered. Make it just a tiny bit larger than the nail.

2. Set piece over the nail and indent with orangewood stick to the shape of the cuticle. Lift the piece off nail and trim to the exact shape of the nail.

3. Apply adhesive to the back of piece and to the nail.

4. Press the bottom of piece to the base of nail and arrange it perfectly to the shape of the nail base. Gently press the rest of the piece down onto the rest of the nail.

5. Smooth with orangewood stick to press out any air bubbles.

6. Use scissors to trim excess from the edges of nail.

7. Seal it with several layers of clear polish making sure the edges are well covered. Be sure to let each layer dry between applications.

Points to Remember

- Make sure nail polish is dry before applying snakeskin or leather. If it is wet the nail might not dry completely and the leather will peel away at the edges or become displaced if touched.

- Trim edges of leather or snakeskin as close as possible so they do not lift or peel away from the nail edges.

- Cover completely with several layers of clear polish making sure the leather or snakeskin is buried in the clear polish. Let each coat dry sufficiently.

- If applying nail tape over design, put it on before covering nail with clear polish. If applying nail gems, wait until just before the last layer of clear polish is to be applied. This will keep the gem from being buried too deep in the clear polish and losing its shine.

18 THREE-DIMENSIONAL, OR 3-D, NAIL ART

Using the same acrylic that is used on sculptured nails, tiny sculptures are made over a sculptured nail form. They are made on a nail form so that they curve to fit the nail instead of laying flat. The sculpture can be anything you can think of—like a candy cane for Christmas or a couple of hearts for Valentine's Day. After removing the design from the nail form you can either decorate it with acrylic paint and glue it onto the nail or glue it on the nail and then paint it, depending on what is easier for you.

The following procedures show how to make a few easy designs. At the end of this chapter are photographs of other designs you can make—or try creating your own.

Supplies Needed

Acrylic powder & liquid

Small brushes

Reusable sculptured nail forms

Files and buffers or drill and
    small drill bits

Nail glue

Orangewood stick

Acrylic paint

Tweezers

Preparation

Polish nails in regular manner. Apply top coat and let dry completely. While polish is drying you can make your sculpture. Some sculptures require more time to make and can be made before the clients come in if you know ahead of time what they want.

To save time, make several of the popular designs like hearts or seasonal decorations and keep on hand.

Procedure for Heart Design

A heart is one of the easiest designs to make.

1. Assemble your acrylic, brushes, and a sculptured nail form.

2. Shape the nail form to fit the shape of the client's fingernail. If you're making the design before the client arrives, try to get it as close to her nail shape as possible. If you are making a design for a pinky finger, remember that it has more of a curve than a thumb or ring finger.

3. Hold nail form facing you. Dip a small brush into the acrylic liquid, wipe excess liquid off brush, and dip into acrylic powder making a small ball on end of brush. The ball of acrylic must be dry or it will run and be difficult to shape.

   If the acrylic is too dry, put it on the form then dip the brush very lightly into the liquid and then onto the ball to moisten it.

4. Use the brush to shape the ball into a triangle. (Fig. 18-1) Pat the top to spread it out and wipe the edges to shape the sides.

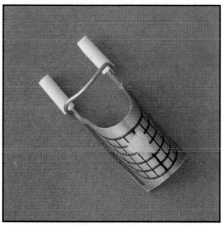

Figure 18-1 Form a triangle to start heart shape.

5. With the orangewood stick, press a small groove in the top of the triangle. Use the brush to shape the round part of the top of the heart. (Fig. 18-2)

6. Let the acrylic dry completely. You can tell if it is dry by tapping on it. A clicking sound indicates it is dry.

7. Finish shaping heart with a file or drill. Smooth the edges.

8. Try heart on for size. If the heart does not fit on the nail properly, try drilling for filing the back of it to flatten it or give it more of a curve, whichever is needed.

9. Apply a small amount of glue to the nail where heart is to be placed.

10. Use tweezers to place heart on the glued area. (Fig. 18-3)

11. Press heart down with an orangewood stick. Do not press too hard or the glue will get squeezed out from under the heart and leave a glue mark on the polish and the heart may not stick on nail completely.

12. Paint heart with acrylic paint in any color you desire. (Fig. 18-4) Try painting T.L., for true love, or the initials of a loved one. You can also enhance the nail with glitter or rhinestones.

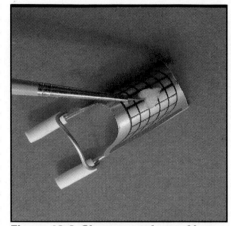

Figure 18-2 Shape round top of heart with tip of brush.

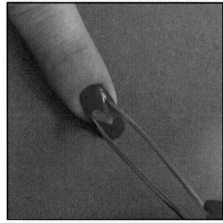

Figure 18-3 Place heart on glued nail area.

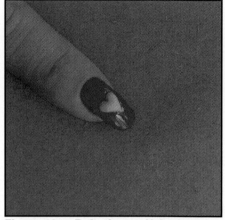

Figure 18-4 Paint heart, if desired.

Figure 18-5 3-D heart design covered with clear polish

13. After the design is dry, cover the entire nail with clear polish to shine and seal. Apply the clear polish slowly and gently to avoid making air bubbles. (Fig. 18-5)

Points to Remember

- A reusable nail form will hold the shape better than a disposable nail form.

- Make sure the form is as close as possible to the shape of the nail the sculpture is going to be put on so the sculpture fits as flat on the nail as possible.

- File or buff the edges of the sculpture before gluing it to the nail so it looks finished and does not have sharp edges to get caught on things.

- Do not put too much glue on the nail when gluing the sculpture or it will squash out from under the sculpture and make the nail art look messy.

- The nail polish must be dry before gluing the sculpture to nail.

- When you are finished painting the nail and decorating the design, cover nail slowly with clear polish to avoid air bubbles in polish.

Figures 18-6–18-9 show different 3-D nail designs you can make. you can also use them for ideas to make your own. Follow the technique outlined in this chapter for making the sculptures.

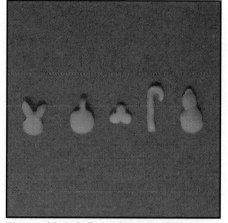

Figure 18-6 3-D sculptures: bunny head, pumpkin, holly berry, candy cane, and snowman

Figure 18-8 3-D tree with presents and candy cane with bow

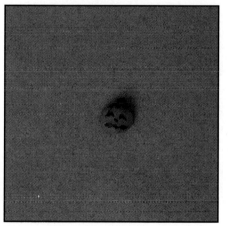

Figure 18-7 3-D painted pumpkin

Figure 18-9 3-D palm tree and butterfly with flowers

19 CONFETTI DECORATION

Confetti is tiny strips of foil that are available in many colors. It can be used alone or with other art mediums to enhance or complete a design. (Fig. 19-1)

Supplies Needed

Confetti

Clear polish

Orangewood stick or tweezers

Preparation

Polish nails in regular manner. Apply top coat and let dry completely.

Procedure

1. Apply clear polish on the nail where the confetti is to be applied. Continue with next step before clear polish dries.

2. Brush small amount of clear polish on end of orangewood stick and touch confetti lightly to pick some up. (Fig. 19-2) You can also use tweezers to apply confetti. (Fig. 19-3) Try both to see what works best for you.

3. Touch the confetti onto the clear polish and it will stick. You can cluster it or apply singularly to create or finish a design.

4. Clean end of orangewood stick with polish remover.

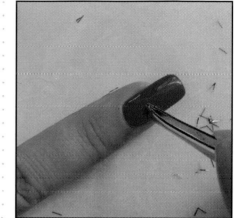

Figure 19-3 You can also use tweezers to apply confetti.

5. Use flat side of stick and gently press the confetti down onto nail.

6. Cover with clear nail polish slowly to avoid air bubbles in polish. Let dry. Apply a second coat of polish to completely seal design.

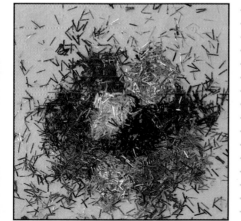

Figure 19-1 Confetti

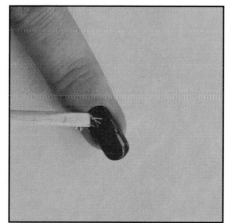

Figure 19-2 Apply confetti with orangewood stick.

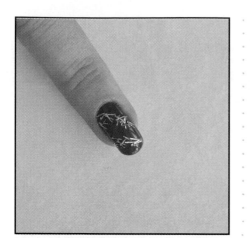

Figure 19-4 Gold confetti on red base

Figure 19-5 Multicolored confetti on pink base

Figures 19-4 and 19-5 illustrate possible confetti designs.

Points to Remember

• Let nail polish dry before starting design or the confetti will mush into polish and look messy.

• Do not let clear polish build up on orangewood stick or the confetti will not come off and stick to nail.

• Be sure the clear polish on nail is wet enough for confetti to stick to.

• Press all the confetti onto the nail so it is flat and does not stick up.

20 FOIL ART

Foil is fun to use for decorating nails. Each time you make a design it comes out differently. To make two nails exactly alike is impossible, but you can make them similar by using the same technique on each nail.

The foil is on a thin cellophane backing. A special emulsion glue is painted on the area of the nail where you want the foil. After the glue is dry, the foil is pressed onto the nail and the cellophane backing is peeled away.

The following explains how to apply the foil. You can use foil alone or with other nail art techniques.

Supplies Needed

Foil in desired color or colors

Emulsion glue

Small scissors

Orangewood stick

Preparation

Paint nails in regular manner. Apply top coat and let dry completely. If nail polish is not dry the foil process will not work.

Procedure

1. Apply emulsion glue to nail you want to cover. (Fig. 20-1)

2. Let glue dry just until it turns clear.

3. Cut a piece of foil and gently press onto the glue. (Fig. 20-2) Pull foil off the nail. The color will adhere to the emulsion, and the cellophane backing will be clear.

4. If you want to add another color, you can press it over the same area to blend the colors. The foil will stick to the glue where the first color did not. (Fig. 20-3)

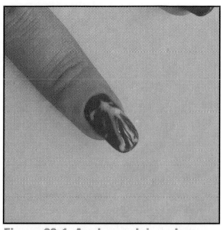

Figure 20-1 Apply emulsion glue.

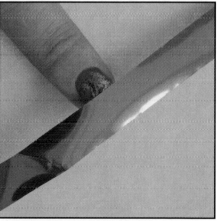

Figure 20-2 Press foil onto glued nail area.

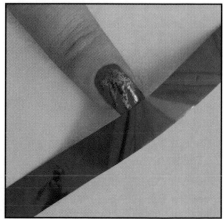

Figure 20-3 Use second color of foil.

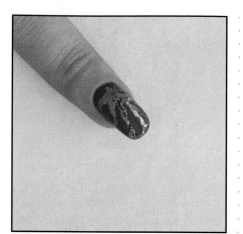

Figure 20-4 Foil design covered with polish

Figure 20-6 Black, silver, and gold foil design

Figure 20-8 Fourth of July designs

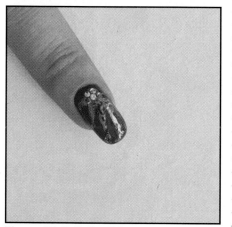

Figure 20-5 Foil with gems

Figure 20-7 Silver, pink, and light pink foil design

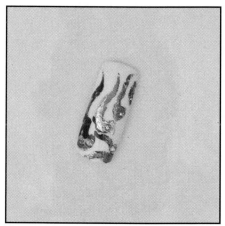

Figure 20-9 Fancy foil art

5. Cover design with clear polish to seal and protect. (Fig. 20-4)

To make fancy designs you can add more emulsion to different areas of the nail and add other colors separately. Bullion beads or gemstones will add to the beauty of the art medium. Figures 20-5–20-9 are examples of different designs made with foil.

21 FREEHAND PAINTING

Freehand painting can be simple or detailed. You can paint flowers by using little dots or paint an ocean scene with rocks and palm trees. Acrylic paint is the best to use because it covers well and rinses out easily with water. Try something simple first and then try to do something a little more complicated. Remember that all artists have their own technique so no two paintings will be alike. If your work is not exactly the same as the painting or picture you are copying it is okay. Use your individualism to create your own style.

Supplies Needed

Acrylic paint

Small sable brushes

Cup of water

Paper towels

Palette on which to mix paint

Orangewood stick

Clear polish

Preparation

Polish nails in regular manner. Apply top coat and let dry.

Procedure for Flower Design

1. Using an orangewood stick place a small amount of color on palette.

2. Dip a small brush into water to moisten the bristles.

3. Dip brush in paint.

4. Make a circle of small dots on nail, then put one dot in the middle. To make several flowers use the same process but make some smaller and some larger.

5. Use a striping brush to make the stems.

6. Let the paint dry completely before applying the clear polish. When applying the clear polish, be sure the brush is wet enough to cover the nail. If there is not enough polish on the brush it can damage your painting by smearing the paint instead of covering it.

Figure 21-1 Gold flowers with bullion beads

You can make the flowers the same color or different colors. In the picture shown here the flowers are done entirely in gold paint with gold bullion beads in the center of each flower. (Fig. 21-1)

You can make the same design with less flowers. Paint them in any color and add green stems. Use you imagination to create your own flower design.

Procedure for Painting a Small Picture

To make a painting you must first block in the background. Add the foreground shapes and then the detail. The following bookworm painting illustrates this technique.

1. Using a medium-size brush, block in the background. In this case the background is the blue book and the white edges for the paper.

2. Paint in the worm and the white hole it is coming out of.

3. Use a tiny brush to finish. Use black paint to detail the painting by outlining the book and worm.

4. Paint the face on the worm and a few stripes on the white to indicate pages. Paint the title of the book. "Math" is used here, but you can make up your own. (Fig. 21-2)

Figure 21-2 Beginning steps and completed bookworm design

5. Let paint dry completely.

6. Carefully cover with clear polish.

Procedure for Painting a Red Sky with Palm Tree and Water

1. Polish nails in regular manner with red polish and let dry.

2. Use a medium-size brush to paint the black land ¼ of the way up the nail.

3. Paint the blue water on bottom of nail and let it overlap the land a little.

4. Paint the yellow sun in the sky off to one side. Let the sun dry before continuing.

5. Use a striping brush or very small brush to paint the black tree trunks and then the tree limbs.

6. Let paint dry completely.

8. Carefully cover with clear polish. (Fig. 21-3)

If you want to make the painting fancy you can add a tiny bit of glitter to the water and on the sun.

Figure 21-3 In-progress and completed red sky with palm tree design

Procedure for Painting an Ocean Scene with Rocks and Palm Tree

1. Paint the upper half of nail light blue and the lower half aqua. To make the water look more real add a little light blue over the aqua.

2. Use white paint to make a couple of clouds.

3. Mix black and white together to make grey for the rocks. Paint them on one side on bottom of nail and on the water line where the sky and water meet. Extend the rocks out a little on the top for an island effect. You can enhance the rocks by adding a little lighter grey over the dark grey. This adds depth to the painting. (Fig. 21-4)

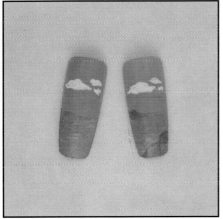

Figure 21-4 In-progress ocean scene

4. Let this dry a couple of minutes before going on.

5. Make the sun with yellow paint and then blend a little orange around the outside to give it a glow.

6. Use a tiny brush and white paint to create the waves splashing on the rocks. If you make the waves too big you can fix them by adding more blue or aqua to cover them up or blend them into the water.

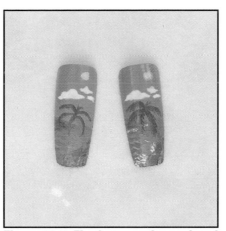

Figure 21-5 Final step and completed ocean scene

7. Use brown paint to make trunk of tree on the front rock. Try mixing your own shade instead of using plain brown.

8. Use dark green to paint the palms, then use a tiny brush to make the small leaves on the palm branches. (Fig. 21-5)

9. Let dry completely and cover with clear polish. You can cover the painting twice to be sure it is sealed under the top coat and won't wear off. Make sure the first coat dries before adding the second coat, or it will not dry completely before the client leaves. With this much work put into a design you do not want the client to smudge the nail.

Making hand-painted designs if fun. You can come up with ideas by using holiday themes. Paint a turkey for Thanksgiving or a candy cane, Christmas tree, or holly leaves for Christmas. For Easter you can paint bunnies or Easter eggs. Use hearts for Valentine's Day and pumpkins or ghosts for Halloween. The Fourth of July gets flags or sparkles for fireworks.

When making any of these designs, you can change the color or design to make it your own.

Special events are a great theme for paintings also. Try a football or the logo of a favorite team for Super Bowl.

Careers can be a source of ideas as well. You can paint the medical emblem for doctors and nurses or a bookworm for a student.

Use your imagination and create your own designs, or let your customers suggest ideas. Don't be afraid to try anything; if you mess up, try it again.

You can practice new designs on nail tips before trying them on a customer. Chapter 23 shows how to do sample or practice nails.

22 COMBINING NAIL ART TECHNIQUES

You can use any nail art medium alone or combine two or more to create beautiful designs. Try covering the nail with lace and then putting a couple of small strips of snakeskin in one corner. You an mix glitter and confetti to make a sparkling design. Enhance hand paintings by mixing some glitter in clear polish and painting it over parts of the picture. Use bullion beads to circle gemstones or sprinkle on a feather design. Be creative and try something new. If you find small items that can be used to do nail design, try them. Designs do not have to come from this book—they can come from you.

Figures 22-1 – 22-3 show different combinations of nail art designs from simple to elaborate.

Figure 22-1 3-D butterfly with flowers and a touch of glitter

Figure 22-3 Gold leaf and gems, foil with gems and bullion beads, feathers with gold leaf and bullion beads

Figure 22-2   The elegance of gold tape, bullion beads, and red gems.

PART
THREE

*Promoting and Selling
Your Nail Art Designs*

PART THREE

Promoting and Selling Your Nail Art Designs

INTRODUCTION

Now that you know how to create a vast array of nail designs, you need to let your customers see what you can do. Setting up attractive displays helps your clients understand some of the many design options available to them and helps to promote your work. Nail design sample displays are selling tools.

•

Another aspect of promoting your work is determining price ranges and packages with which you are comfortable. When you establish fair prices without selling yourself short, you actually increase your customers' confidence in you. They'll know that you value your work as much as they do.

•

The final chapter in this book offers a pictorial essay of nail art. Take a look and have fun creating your own designs.

23 MAKING DESIGN SAMPLES

To make sample designs or practice nail art you simply use a nail tip, an orangewood stick, and some acrylic.

First file the end of the nail tip to smooth it. File the number off and buff the spot so it is smooth. Doing this first will make your nail art sample look neat, and there will not be any scratches under the polish.

Turn the nail tip over and place it on the table. Put a small ball of acrylic on the end of the nail tip and place the tip of an orangewood stick into acrylic. Let it lay there until it is dry. When the acrylic is dry you can hold the stick with the nail on it to make your nail art sample or to practice making designs. (You can also use nail glue to attach the stick on the nail tip, but it does not hold as well as the acrylic.)

Follow the instructions for the nail design you want to learn. Try combining several techniques to make your own designs. The more sample nails you have to show your customers, the more nail art you will sell.

Figures 23-1–23-5 are samples of combination nail designs fastened to orangewood sticks.

Figure 23-1 Handpainted flowers and gemstones with confetti

Figure 23-3 3-D nail art snowman and ghost

Figure 23-2 Handpainted nail art samples

Figure 23-4 Feather with bullion beads and a glitter design

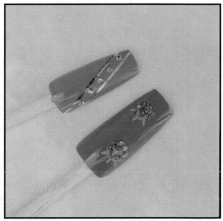

Figure 23-5 Gemstone designs

24 DISPLAY YOUR WORK

After you have some nail art samples made you must put them out where your customers can see them all the time. They may not want the designs the first or second time they come in, but if they see the display every time they have their nails done eventually they will start asking you if you can do something for them. Be sure to tell them that they do not have to choose from your display. You can't possibly have every nail design you can make on display because the possibilities are endless. Also, let your customers know that any design can be changed to their liking.

So get your work out on display so your customers and start thinking about what they want. Some customers will ask for exactly what they see or they will want the design you are wearing.

Make or purchase a stand that holds the nail sticks in rows so they can be looked at easily. The stand works well because the nails all face front and can be arranged by category for a smart-looking display. (Fig. 24-1) You can also arrange your nail sticks in a pretty glass jar or vase using glass floral balls to hold the nail sticks in place so they can be seen.

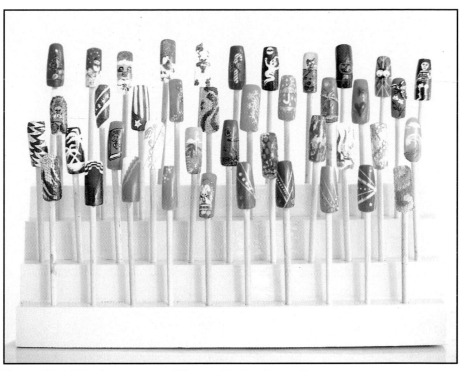

Figure 24-1 Display as many different kinds of sample designs as you can in your nail art stand.

25 SETTING PRICES

When charging for your nail art you must take into account the time and talent put into your work. Even if it is easy and fun for you it is work. Some people could not begin to make designs or paint art on paper much less on a tiny fingernail.

Don't undersell yourself. Most nail art should start at $1 for each nail for a simple design such as a French manicure (Fig. 25-1) or gold stripes with gemstones. (Fig. 25-2) If the design entails more work and more time, the price goes up. The harder the design the higher the price. If a customer wants the same design on every nail instead of on each hand you an bring the price down a little because they are getting more.

For example, a lace design over the corner of one nail with confetti or bullion beads trimming the lace can cost $3. If the customer wants the same design on all ten nails you can charge $20 for the work (that's $2 per nail instead of $3).

For 3-D nail art you should charge at least $4 for a candy cane or a heart and more money for holly leaves with berries. A Christmas tree with packages under it can cost up to $10 a nail depending on how fancy you get. (Fig. 25-3)

Remember to discuss prices with your customers *before* you start so there are no misunderstandings after the work is done.

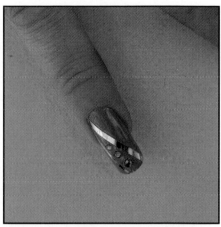

Figure 25-2 Inexpensive gold tape and gemstones design

Figure 25-1 A French manicure can be at the beginning of your price range.

Figure 25-3 You can charge more for intricate designs.

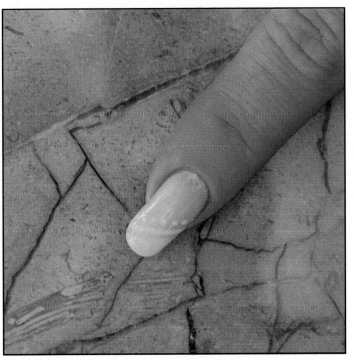

Figure 26-1 Fancy French manicure

Figure 26-2 Design for doctor or nurse

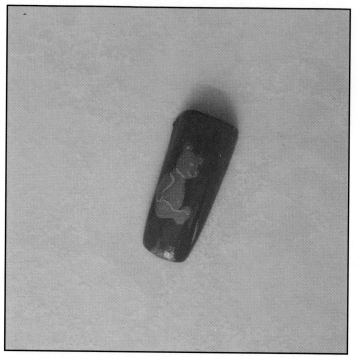

Figure 26-3 Lavender bear

Figure 26-4 Lace and leather, black and silver snakeskin

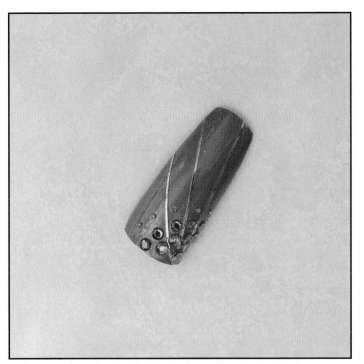

Figure 26-5 Nail tape with gems and bullion beads

Figure 26-6 3-D palm tree, painted trees with glitter, and a wave with glitter

Figure 26-7 Nail tape and silver beads

Figure 26-8 3-D rainshower nail, 3-D hearts

Figure 26-9 Pierced nail charm

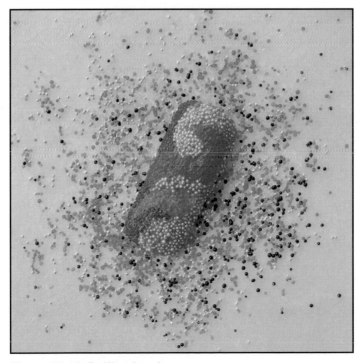

Figure 26-10 Bullion beads

Figure 26-11 Bullion beads

Figure 26-12 Bullion beads

Figure 26-13 Snakeskin nails on snakeskin

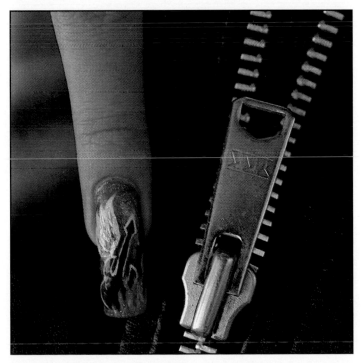

Figure 26-14 Angel wing and fire on a guitar

Figure 26-15 Glitter nails holding gold bottle

Figure 26-16 Feather art and necklace

Figure 26-17 Hot pink and gems

INDEX